Poets Centre Stage

Volume Two

By

(In order of appearance)

Gerald Morgan
Dawn Alexander
Jim Wild
David Marland
Sandra Rowell
Alan Barker
Andrew Powell

Published by

Cauliay Publishing & Distribution

PO Box 12076
Aberdeen
AB16 9AL
www.cauliaypublishing.com

First Edition

ISBN 978-0-9558992-3-2

Copyright © The Poets

Front cover design © Cauliay Publishing

A CIP catalogue record for this book is available from the
British Library.

Introduction

The idea behind Poets Centre Stage was conceived back in 2006 when I realised that there was too great a void between writers and their audience. Even today only 2% of writers' work is ever seen by the general public, the remainder sadly is either left in the writer's study having been rejected by publishers often without being read, or it is never sent away in the first place because most writers know the futility of casting their net into an empty sea. Speaking of Futility the great First World War poet Wilfred Owen was once asked what he was fighting for his answer was simple yet powerful enough to make the whole world stop and think: "I am fighting for the English Language." Cauliay Publishing was established to try to redress the unacceptable imbalance between what is written and what is read by giving just those few more talented people the opportunity to see their work in print. Here is a collection of poetry that any publisher would be proud to put before an audience hungry for originality and entertainment. We have produced an anthology as rich in imagery as it is in unspoilt beauty. The myriad of emotions expressed in each lovingly created poem clearly reflect those most honourable ideals of Wilfred Owen and all the brave men and women who fought and died to maintain them.

Michael William Molden
August 2008.

Gerald Morgan

I was born in Girvan, South Ayrshire on the 28th of March 1954, and have stayed in the town all my life. I met my wife to be, Gina, in 1969 and we married in 1974. We have one daughter Sara, who came along in 1981.

I first started dabbling with writing in my late teens, and have continued in a stop start fashion ever since.

My first piece of work was *Balshazer The Cod* – one hundred and fifty four lines of rhyming couplets which tell the tale of a little fish who embarks on an amazing adventure. The birth of my grandson Daniel in 2002 was my motivation to turn *Balshazer* into a short story for children.

I tend to write "off the cuff" rather than in any structured fashion, and my work encompasses a variety of styles, subjects and moods.

Among my favourite poets are Robert Burns, Roger McGough and Spike Milligan – with a special place for the lyrics of Bob Dylan.

Stirling – 13.07.01

Six forty five and the queue is fast growing.
Anticipation's high.
And the atmosphere's grand.

Zimmy and the boys are plucking and blowing.
Their sound check just teasing,
The gathering band.

Starting to move and the excitement is flowing.
Ages ranging,
From A to Zee.

Just a bit further then the stage lights are glowing.
Another half hour,
And then Bobby D.

Waiting and watching till some outlines are showing.
Is that the man
From the far northern land?

Acoustic strings sound then the harp is a' blowing.
Ecstatic crowd,
In the palm of his hand.

Fourteen song set with the people all knowing.
It may be the last.
They'll see the man play.

Encores galore – like a party he's throwing.
Is he saying goodbye,
In his own unique way?

Billy Mackenzie

I never knew Billy.
I wish I had.
Not to tell him, not to guide him, not to lecture him.

I wish I'd known Billy.
For only ten seconds.
Or six.
Or one!

I wish I knew Billy, when it mattered.
For just one second.

Just to say no!

Alexander Tudhope

Who will weep in years to come?
Whose tears will well and run?
For Alexander Tudhope.
A brother and a son.

Who will say, with family pride,
"A hero's work was done?"
By Alexander Tudhope.
A brother and a son.

Who made the call too soon,
And left no time to run?
Poor Alexander Tudhope.
A brother and a son.

Not taken by the enemy's fire.
Not taken by a gun.
Brave Alexander Tudhope.
A brother and a son.

And so he lies in foreign earth,
Beneath the Gallic sun.
Dear Alexander Tudhope.
A brother and a son.

So, who will weep in years to come?
Whose tears will well and run?
For Alexander Tudhope.
A brother and a son.

Defying Nature

Blues music is cool.
Even when it's hot! Hot! Hot!
Down in the Delta.

Autumn Leaves – A Song for Gina

Autumn leaves fall silently
And winter darkness creeps
And we make love uncaringly
While summer drifts to sleep.

And all the world just passes by
Outside our daydream paradise
And nothing can disturb our thoughts
The seasons drift on by.

We see the spring in each others eyes
Sunshine fills our minds
The cold damp wind of worried times
Has faded far behind.

And we keep loving on and on
Inside our daydream paradise
And while we stay so much in love
The seasons drift on by.

July will come when June is gone
As June will follow May
But month by month and year by year
We'll make love every day.

The wind and rain won't leave us cold
The frost and snow won't bite
And we'll need nothing but ourselves
To take us through the night.

And we ask nothing of the world
Except our daydream paradise
And while our love goes on unchanged
The seasons drift on by.

Farewell to Girvan

Take me back to Girvan shore
That I may rest my gaze
On Arran, Kintyre and Ailsa Craig
And remember happy days.

Take me to The Old Mill Road
Running by The Byne
And let me see her craggy face
For auld lang syne.

Take me to Knockcushion Hill
Where kings before me stood
And let me see Old Stumpy Tower
To recall happy times and good.

Take me to my old school gates.
And let me wait a while
Until the memories unlock
And bring to me a smile.

Take me back to Girvan please
That I may say farewell
To all the special sights and scenes
Of which you've heard me tell.

Moonface and Will O' The Wisp

Riding south on the Silver Line,
Cold north rain at our backs.
While Moonface and Will O' The Wisp
Dance above our tracks.

Past Brussels, through Bavaria,
With Zimmy on the phones.
Bedding down to the mountain sounds
To rest our weary bones.

Alpine streams, so crystal clear,
Meander and cascade.
While the crags and peaks stand tall and proud –
Magnificence God made.

Pretty gasthofs decked with bloom,
Offer hospitality.
Then, rested, we are moving on – my love,
Gina, and me.

To Brenner, Innsbruk, Europa bridge,
Through tunnels by the score.
Our destination drawing close
Now just a few hours more.

Soon landscapes change to rolling hills,
Resplendent with the vine.
Olive groves and cypress trees
The land of fine fine wine.

Village roofs of terracotta,
And brightly coloured walls.
Picture postcard Tuscan scenes
The traveller enthrals.

Now we're there and settled in,
Ready to explore.
Florence, Pisa, Sienna town
And Elba's stunning shore.

San Gimignano's many towers,
Steeped in history.
The Florence baptistery ceiling works
So wonderful to see.

All too soon it's time to go,
Back to the north country.
And leave behind this place we love
Gina and me.

Riding north on the Silver Line,
Warm south sun at our backs,
And Moonface and Will O' The Wisp
Still dance above our tracks.

Kate's Tale – The Real Story of Tam O'Shanter

Pare Kate, a humble honest sowl
Wha ne'er abody had e'er seen scowl
Wha reared her bairns wi' great devotion
For her ain well bein' she'd ne'er a notion.

Fine Kate, wha widnae herm a flea
Wha cared for a' things big or wee
Wha'd help her neebors when they came
Tae beg the last coin tae her name.

Kind Kate, wha kept her hame sae smert
Wha hud the gid o' aw at hert
Wha went tae Kirk an' prayed for ithers
Weans an' man an' freens an' brithers.

But Kate, she nursed a simmerin' fear
For her man Tam – wha she loved dear
He liked tae drink wi freens the nappy
Until they a' got unco happy.

Tam, for weeks on end wid sup
Wi' cronies keen tae tak a cup
While Kate, wid sit at hame an' wunner
When he'd finally take the scunner.

The money made fae merket sales
Wid disappear on wines an' ales
While his weans made dae wi' crusts a while
Tam wined an' dined in jaunty style.

Kate began tae form a plan
Tae frichten her misguided man
She'd tell him that she'd hud a dream
That saw him face doon in the stream.

Wi' water lappin' ower his back
While up abin, the boughs did crack
As lichtenin' struck wi' a' it's micht
An' lit the sky wi' powerful licht.

As witches, warlocks auld an' knarled
Poked an' prodded, screamed an' snarled
An' cursed his name as he lay still
Ablow the water near the mill.

But Kate could no' hae been prepared
Fur whit came nixt an' made her scared
When through her thochts – made up ye mind
She unleashed power o' an evil kind.

As she sat starin' at the fire's flame
An' thocht that this wid bring Tam hame
The de'il himsel' wis takin' heed
O' pare sad Kate's fictitious deed.

For unbeknown tae Kate hersel'
Auld Nick wid pick up thochts an' tell
His trusted servants, dark an' grim
Tae set in place a trap for him.

Tae lure auld Tam fae aff his path
Tae Alloway Kirk tae feel his wrath
As he fae Ayr wid shin set oot
On Meg, his mount sae fleet o' foot.

Noo Tam had taen a fill himsel'
So pide his dues an' bade farewell
Tae Soutar Johnnie his trusted frien
(Mare loyal man there'd never been).

Tam turned aboot an' stepped ootside
Tae where his gid steed Meg did bide.
Then efter feedin' her wae straw
He mounted her and was awa.

Feelin' happy fae the drink
Tam sang and whistled - and did think
Aboot his Kate and his warm bed
Wae nae idea whit lay ahead.

Tam spurred on Meg tae gallop west
Then south towards his hame, an' rest
Through gorse an' thistle at a thunnerin' gait
Oblivious tae his dreadful fate.

Noo Kate, retired fur the night
Wis restless, fearful o' Tam's plight
Driftin' in a fretful sleep
She dreamt a dream that made her weep.

She saw her Tam, his eyes agog
Emergin' fae a rotten bog
Drippin' wet and caked wi' glaur
While letting forth an anguished lor.

His coat wi' torn an' tattered threads
Hung aff his back in matted shreds
His calicos, wance unco smert
Were ripped tae bits an' torn apert.

His face wis etched wi' pain an' fear
Distorted, twisted ear tae ear
He shook as if in frantic fit
His blid dreept fae a gapin' slit.

Kate saw in her mind's eye unfold
A sicht which made her blid rin cold
Towerin' high ower Tam's wrecked frame
Stood Lucifer – with eyes aflame.

An' all aboot his evil form
Stood witches, warlocks – like a swarm
Each chantin' in an eerie howl
"Rip him up fae cheek tae jowel."

Screamin' banshees could ne'er surpass
The murderous screams o' this wicked mass
They bayed fur blid an' grisly gore
Then fae Nick himsel' there came a roar.

Sae loud an' shrill his ain kind ceased
An' turned towards the michty beast.
He held aloft a torch of fire
An' by his side their stood a pyre.

Prepared fur Tam – his helpless prey
Wha for his deeds was shin tae pay
A drastic, hideous, final fee
Burned alive an' left tae dee.

Noo a' this time Kate turned an' tossed
An' fretted ower the man she'd lost
Her Tam, whose face now filled her thoughts
Wis gid an' kind fur a' his fauts.

An honest man – a man o' pride
A man she wanted by her side
A kind an' gentle faither tae
"Oh dearest Tam, whit did they dae?"

Jist then Kate came roon tae hear
A sound, familiar tae her ear.
The sound o' hoofs on cobbled stane
Then a latch bein' raised and drapped again.

Tam was back fae his lang days toil
O' ploughin' fields an' tillin' soil.
An' Kate noo stirred an' came tae see
That aw wis weel, as things should be.

Balshazer the Cod

Golden rays on summer nights
Sunset o'er the sea, which lights
The fishes homes, below the waves
Honest fishes and fishy naves
Now a story of one such fish I'll tell
Balshazer the Cod whom I knew well
He lived alone between two rocks
His home was furnished with chairs and clocks
And in the cranny 'neath his front door
Balshazer stored his food and more
This cranny held his socks and shoes
His Sunday suit and hunting trews
His violin and sweeper too
Not to mention his coat of blue
But enough's been said about his hoard
I mustn't let you get too bored
So now I will recite my tale
Of Balshazer's adventures in the land called Zail
One summer morning as Balshazer swam
He came across a massive dam
And try as hard as he might
He could not conquer such a height.
And as he turned towards his home
He heard a rather frightening groan.
"That was no fish" said Balshazer quaking.
"Why, it has the whole earth shaking".

"Good day young cod" came the deep strong voice.
"Did I startle you with my noise?"
"A little" said Balshazer turning pale.
And spinning round, he saw the whale.
Balshazer had never seen a whale before
Except in a book kept below his front door.
"I'm called Balshazer", said our hero.
Nephew of Cod Raefus Nero.
"Ah!" said the whale smiling freely.
"Nephew of Raefus" are you really?"
"My name my frightened little fellow
is Franklin Colbert James Othello.
Now would you like a helping hand
To get across this mass of sand"
"Yes please" replied Balshazer with haste.
"I'd really love to explore that place.
You see, excitement's what I seek
So I've locked my house up for a week.
I've put out the trash and cancelled the milk
Drawn the blinds and curtains of silk"
"May I interrupt", said Franklin O
"Please jump on by back for I must go
I've got a date for half past nine
And I would like to look real fine
So please be quick, no time to waste
I'll get you over with the greatest of haste"
At this Balshazer mounted the whale
And was struck quite soundly by Franklin's tail
He soared up high across the wall
Then felt himself begin to fall
He must have dropped ten feet or more
Then landed on some foreign shore.

Balshazer was amazed at what he saw
Huge green fields with stacks of straw
He saw some geese fly overhead
And in the distance a small green shed.
Balshazer moved towards the hut
But sadly the door was tightly shut,
So, standing up on his tail fin
He reached the window and peered in
Inside there was a table neatly laid
And beside the stove some Scottish Maid
"My favourite butter, Oh lovely" said he
"But how can I get it when I have no key
I must try and break the window pane
Or the sight of that butter will drive me insane"
Finding a stick in the nearby grass
Balshazer struck and broke the glass
He dragged himself through the wooden frame
And made towards his tasty game
Reaching out he grabbed the pray
Thinking it was his lucky day
But getting the butter was not so easy
Because, being warm, it was rather greasy
It slipped from his grasp and fell to the floor
And before he could catch it, it went under the door
It rolled by hill and river and dale
Until it reached the Mountain of Zail
Reaching the mountain, Balshazer cried
"As Nero's my uncle I'll have you fried
Just then an elf came down the hill
Of Balshazer's noise he'd had his fill.

"What's this row," he cried with rage
"Can't I have some peace in this day and age
I've got to get my daily snooze
But one hour a day I seem to lose
I settled down at half past ten
Its now eleven and I'm up again
Now please explain your unruly behaviour
A good excuse will be your saviour
On hearing this, Balshazer shook
He'd read of elves in his reference book
"Nasty creatures" he remembered well
"Oh dear what story can I tell
To save myself from his elfin wrath
If I make a mistake he'll cut me in half."
"Well elfin sir", he said aloud.
"I was passing on that large white cloud
And from above an eagle flew
And from its scabbard my sword I drew
But the king of birds was far too cunning
I felt a blow which was quite stunning
I somersaulted through the air
And landed head first over there.
So now, you see, my elfin friend
I almost met a nasty end."
Before Balshazer uttered another sound
He found himself flat on the ground
"You lie." cried the elf whose name was Caeser
"You must think I'm a gullible geezer
But I'm very smart although I'm old
And I don't believe one word you've told
Liars in this land are punished by hanging
And the same applies to beings caught slanging
So you will be hung when the dawn breaks tomorrow
Ah! I see by your face you are filled with sorrow"
Balshazer was stunned by the elfs harsh sentence

And got on his knees to beg Caesers repentance
"Please spare me good sir" cried the cod in distress
"Oh how did I ever get into this mess
I just wanted adventure, excitement and fun
I hoped for all three but I'm going to get none
Just then three more ageing elves appeared
Each with a hat and also a beard
"Good Caeser" cried the oldest fellow
"Did you know that the cod has spoken with Othello"
"Othello?" answered Caeser, calmer by now
And pushed his hat back from his brow
"If I had known this ten minutes ago
I would not have put on such a show
Othello indeed! This is very odd
Why should Othello converse with a Cod?"
By now Balshazer had dried his eyes
And had decided to tell no more lies
"I'll tell you the truth if you'll bear with me
It's a rather long story as you will see"
So Balshazer told the elves his tale
Of how he chased the butter over hill and dale
Now the elves were greatly impressed by his story
And took him to their town in glory
Where to this day, Balshazer the Cod
Has lived the life of a Mountain God
He remembers his home between the rocks
His furniture and his ticking clocks
His Sunday suit which he needs no more
And his little cranny beneath the door
But he knows he's a very lucky fellow
Just because he met Othello.

The Loss

On the side of a hill a good friend was laid,
In a coffin of pine, and I stared.
At the men and the women who gathered to mourn,
And pray to their God who was there.

I looked all around me at faces in black,
And I wondered how few would survive.
When - maybe tomorrow – death's knock would appear,
And their time to be boxed would arrive.

There were men. There were boys. There were young and
some old,
But the expression on each was the same.
Grief stricken faces all bonded by death,
And all shocked at how sudden it came.

Strong men stood weeping for the death of a friend,
And the widow was numbed by the pain.
And the fatherless children grew up overnight.
They'd never be children again.

The rain on the hills ran in tears of respect,
And the grey clouds all blocked out the sun.
And the chill in the wind cut through to the skin,
Then the service was over and done.

I watched and I listened as the gathering split,
And they made their way back from the grave.
And the long saddened faces said nothing at all,
Just thankful that they had been saved.

Tunnel Vision

Moods, which mirror the black expanse
Of a mid winter sky,
Dredge thoughts of despair
From the deepest recesses of the mind.
No spark. No hope or ray of light
To raise the drowning spirit.
The burden, buried within,
But carried, like a ball and chain,
Drags downward on a never ending spiral.
The inner silence screams.
An unheard cry for help.
Driving home it's message
Of anguish and of pain.
An empty existence.
A pointless journey, it seems,
Will last forever.
And the endless tunnel
Offers no prospect of escape.

Yes Sir – No Sir

Your spiteful acid tongue swells up, to fill your empty mind.
Cutting words of hate you spit, to gratify your kind.

With a head full of opinions, you're a stranger to the truth.
Bombastic, loud, obnoxious - in a word, uncouth.

I despise your sort, you bully and cajole.
No one measures up (you think), but you're the real asshole.

You surround yourself with sycophants, who jump to do your
bidding.
Yes sir, no sir, and three bags full sir - who do you think
you're kidding?

Please crawl back beneath your stone, you and your wicked
mind.
One day your spiteful tongue will swell, and choke you and all
your kind.

Dawn Alexander

I am a Complementary Therapist and Healer from Aberdeen. I was certified as an Angel Therapy Practitioner ® by Doreen Virtue, Ph.D., some years ago and brought angels into my life. Angels are 'beings of light' who can assist us in every area of our lives and my role is to channel this angelic assistance to every person who requests it. Being blessed with the gift of Psychic Mediumship I also connect with the spirit world to bring forth messages of love, guidance and validation.

My background prior to this was diverse, ranging from Sales Representative to working with children in a crèche. During those years I felt like I was constantly searching for the missing piece of the puzzle to my happiness and inner peace. This inner turmoil that surfaced at intervals throughout my life has been a source of inspiration for my writing. Expressing my thoughts, feelings, hopes and dreams through my poetry is a healing and enlightening process. I am a mum to Robbie: my own angel brought into my life to provide me with an added dimension to life and another piece of the puzzle. I now see life as a continual quest for knowledge, expansion and self-discovery. Having found my divine life purpose I will continue to use the medium of poetry to channel messages of love and wisdom from the angels as well as sharing my life experience through verse.

I hope that my words will touch you in some way and will inspire you to embrace your own inner angel.

Who am I?

The tears fall from my heart
My eyes are black and blue
My lips are cold and lonely
My heart is weary too

The pain runs through my chest
The joy runs out of my veins
Energy seeps from my muscles
Confusion reigns in my soul

Lord; Lift me out of this
Help me see the light once more
Open my heart to divine love
See the strength in me

My conviction, addiction
A thirst for love and knowledge
Tenderness and support
A frightened child wants to be loved

Magical Moon

Moon energy awash
The tides ebb and flow
Light on the pebbles
Sparkles in the sky

Moonbeams on sand grains
Seaweed silvery strands
Oceans of love alight
The goddess energy alive

Radiating and generating
Dolphin energy abound
Sonic systems vibrate
Love emanating from the light

Glowing shades of white
Rainbow colours appear
Prisms of energy's song
Awakening the night

Divinity

The veil has been lifted
Separation no longer apparent
Mist clears, future unfolds
Walking the path of the present

Only a fragment of time in reality
Sectioned by nothing at all
Visible to those who want to see
Ready to embrace your truth

Letting your light shine forth
The power you are ready to show
No longer holding back in fear
Freedom is yours, the path is clear

Acceptance by your soul group
You gravitate towards them now
Saturated by divine love and compassion
Judgement is no longer required

Surrender

In the stillness of the moment
I enjoy just being
Watching the thoughts pass by

In the stillness of the moment
I enjoy not doing
Relaxing every inch of my being

In the noise of the silence
That I am not accustomed to
The ticking clock reverberates

Cars speed past my window
Wind howls through the trees
Echoing the force I feel inside

Anger has been uncovered
Control, I thought I had
Should have put my foot on the brake

My head pounds with guilt
My eyes sting with the tears
I know what it's like to be scared

Pain stabs through my heart
I have to let it go
Surrendering and a plea for help

Many Worlds

Confusion seclusion
Heart hurts and head
Mixed signals on air
Blocking out the reality

Tuning into the set
Of soul system star person
Realisation of separation
Unification and personification

Galaxies around observing
Penetrating our midst, unseen
Filtrating the blood of humanity
Lifting the impurities

Plasma cells, DNA entwined
Strands of evidence uncovered
Magnification and multiplication
Simplicity explained

Dark Souls

Creeping into the flesh
Searching into the soul
Leering into the heart
Encroaching on our life

The dark ones come near
We must slay them with love
No place for them here
Banish that vibration

Replace with light frequency
Transmitted through your cells
Permeating to your core matrix
Energy patterns encoded

Chakra Dance

It starts at the crown
Chakra of shining white
Dances into my body
Fills me up with light

Down through my body
Colours blue to red
I feel warmth surround me
Filling up my head

A fusion of swirling colours
The chakras dance around
This is an inner peace
That I have finally found

Re-balanced at last
My chakras dance within
Is this where my
Spiritual dance begins

Angels

Translucent, Opalescent
Sparkling, Twinkling
Angels in the sky

Shining, Twirling,
Floating and flying
Around us

Caring, Sharing
Knowing, Loving
Angels all around us

Thousands of colours
Merged into one
Light up our lives

Angels, Angels, Angels
Angels in our lives
We say – Thank You!

Melting

It was as if time had stopped
A paralysis
Fear held me back
Scared to take a step

Frozen in ice
Cryogenics
Preserved for the future
Live for today

Sacred is the life
Blessed are we
God's children
Breathe

Open your heart
Live your life
Risk equals joy
Let it flow

Enchantment

Rainbows shine bright
The sky is alive
Look up and inhale
Wonderment

Stars twinkle bright
The sky is alive
Gazing towards
Life's pleasures

God's presence within
Feel the warmth
Surround and enclose
We are alive

Accessible to all
The joy of love
Breathe and live
For eternity

Illumination

A kaleidoscope,
Fusion, swirling
Colours, collage
Mosaic, transparent

Beaming, shining
Glowing, pulsating
The light within
Switches on

Eyes of Innocence

Young child gazes
Out at the world
Eyes of innocence
Carefree spirit

Run free child
Spread your wings
Grow tender seedling
To be nourished always

Gentle touches, loving words
Young child smiles
Mother smiles in return
An eternal love

A Smile

Grey skies turn blue
Rainbows shine
Birds sing in the trees
You make me smile

Music comes alive
Children sing
Captivated by your presence
You make me smile

Meetings with our eyes
A connection
Warm touches by your side
You make me smile

The Volcano

Like a chamber of molten magma
Rising up orange in my sacral chakra
Travelling at great speed upwards
Settling in my solar plexus

A fiery furnace inside
Bubbling and burning within
Been lying dormant for years
Is it now ready to erupt?

The volcano inside, pressure
Pushing upwards, funneling
Smoke filled hollow, flames alight
Burning embers aglow

Your Angel

Looking for comfort
Extend your arms
I'll protect you
From any harm

I'll wrap you up
In my loving wings
Protect you forever
From everything

Enclose you in light
A bubble so white
Strengthen your aura
Increase your might

Who am I?
You may say
If you haven't met me
Along the way

I am your angel
Your friend so true
I am your angel
And I love you

Child Meditation

I entered the room
To see a naked figure
Huddled in a corner
Devoid of love and warmth

I reached out my hand
Led her into the garden
Standing timidly, she froze
Exposed for the entire world to see

I left her briefly and went inside
A young girl skipped out
Cheery, sunny yellow girl
Sunny yellow dress, long hair

The two played together
Their energies entwined
Then I realised that both of them were mine

The Predator

Child huddled in the corner
Afraid to turn around
Sobbing and frightened
Scared she might be found

The predator arrives
She feels his looming presence
The dark aura envelops
Fear is what she can sense

She stays still and waits
Hoping he doesn't see her there
Will he reign his blows again?
To be honest, she doesn't care

Believing that she's somehow bad
This must be the punishment she fears
Is this what I deserve?
No loving words come to her ears

Held back and held down
A cloud of negativity surrounds
Lifting her head up high
A glimmer of hope she has found

Increase the Light

A flickering candle, a light
A flickering candle, so bright
Brighter and stronger it grows
Increasing the light, it shows

Once small but rising high
Magnificent light, to the sky
Increasing the light, it shows
Enlighten the world, we grow

Angelic consciousness, it grows
Belief in angels, it shows
Increasing the light, we believe
What we see and perceive

A knowing inside, we feel
A knowing inside, they're real
Angels inside, we just know
Our love for them still grows

Reaching Out

The day is long but feels even longer
I feel strong but want to feel stronger
I feel pain but want to feel less
I will survive, sort out this mess

Can't you hear what I say?
Listen to me for just one day
I don't mean to hurt, but I feel sad
I don't want to shout, but I feel mad

Open your ears open your heart
I want to love, not to part
I long to live in harmony
Give me your love and protect me

Talk to me, not run and hide
Feel what I feel, look inside
Alone and sad, left behind
Take a look at me, what do you find?

Mother Earth

World in a turmoil
Upside down
Inverted; on its head
Worry all around

Toxins, pollution
It does surround
From the hole in the sky
To the dirt on the ground

Repairing and sharing
Tender love we need
Take caution, start caring
Please follow my lead

Safety

I shelter from the storm
In my place of safety
Inside of myself I know
Is the secret to this place

Hidden from view of others
I crouch and feel the warmth
My cocoon and my haven
Security and stability

My angels I call upon
Provide me with this sanctuary
The everlasting protection
That supports my soul

Jim Wild

Jim Wild is sixty seven years old, recently widowed with two grown up daughters. He also has two grandchildren, a boy and a girl. He was born into a family of four where talking and reading were all part of a normal day. Reading a wide variety of books on differing subjects has always been a great interest to him. His writing influences are many, his grandson for his wonderful enquiring mind and his boundless enthusiasm, his granddaughter for her thoughtfulness and of course his two daughters for their support. Jim has many friends and two friends in particular, Dot and Di, who often help with their respected opinions. Jim also draws on the influence of his late wife who showed him the meaning of love and care. In his own words Jim says: "I will always be grateful to her. She suffered a terrible illness for many years before she died and she bore that illness with immense strength and character. Some of my poetry reflects the feeling of desperation that I felt when her illness was drawing to its bitter end. My wife suffered from Alzheimer's disease and it was almost unbearable to see her change from a bright, breezy lady, full of fun and vigour, to a very poorly lady who became increasingly confused and afraid, finally losing touch with reality.

FACES ARE LIKE POETRY
SOME HAPPY AND SOME SAD
I LIKE THIS FACE YOU GAVE TO ME
IT'S THE NICEST ONE I'VE HAD.

47

Somewhere We'd Been

I went somewhere we'd been before
we strolled along the beach
The boats were pulled up on the sand
Just out of waters reach
We walked around the rocky pools
And danced across the shore
We ate in a secluded cove
and laughed until we were sore

We planned to come again someday
We liked this spot so well
And hoped the magic of this place
Would weave another spell
But when I went t'was not the same
The glow could not be seen
As though the fascination
Had been stolen from the scene

I tried in vain to feel the joy
Alas, I should have known
Last time we strolled together
But this time I was alone

Dream Lady

Have you seen the lady the one who gives out dreams
She drifts around us through the night then vanishes it seems
She always carries with her a sack that's coloured gold
And from the sack she gives out dreams and stories to be told
The lady drifts right through the air not bordered in by walls
And just by touching pillowed heads leaves stories that
enthrall
Old memories come flooding back mixed in with hopes and
plans
And then she drifts away so quiet as if she's cupped in unseen
hands
The lady touches babies and babies start to smile
She strokes their hair and then their cheek just pausing for a
while
And when the babies smile and stretch she slowly passes on
She has a dream, a smile, a touch, for each and everyone
She pauses smiling by the beds of all the girls and boys
And from her sack she gives out dreams of favourite games
and toys
She sees them as they turn and smile and settle in their sleep
The memories and dreams she gives they can forever keep
Sometimes a dream escapes from in its golden case
And wondering alone unseen the dream looks for a place
To spread a little happiness and give its golden glow
To share its special gift of joy the dream must onward go
And if the dream comes right to you whenever night or day
Then let the dream engulf you as it goes along its way
That's how our dreams are made and shared so everyone can
feel
A hope, a dream, a prayer a smile can sometimes be so real

Family Life

We're going to a party soon, my mam our kid and me
I bet that there are some sausage rolls some jelly and some tea
I'll have a bit of everything and seconds if I'm quick
And when I get back home at night I'll probably be sick

The party is for cousin, John; he's not as old as me
At their house they have cakes a lot especially Sunday tea
Sometimes we have bread and jam and sometimes only bread
So sometimes I don't eat at home, but at John's house instead

I wouldn't like to live at John's; his mam is really posh
My dad says she's a show off cause she has a lot of dosh
John hasn't got a brother or a sister of his own
And every night he goes up to his bedroom all alone

I know my brother is a pest he follows me about
And when I want to go to sleep he always seems to shout
I wouldn't swap him for a coat made out of golden thread
For when we snuggle up at night he keeps me warm in bed.

John is very lucky with a holiday each year
There's just him and his mother go, his dad goes on the beer
We have a day trip every year it's always been the same
We play out on the beach all day my dad's in every game

My sisters are both older and they are pretty tough
And if I need protection they can be pretty rough
They fight in pairs and two of them put bigger lads to fight
You feel quite safe with them around whenever day or night

My mam's a little woman but she is very strong
She lands a hefty smack if she things that you've done wrong
But when she thinks you're poorly then she makes a smashing
nurse
But she looks really sad when she has nothing in her purse

I think that I am lucky to have a family so good
And those that haven't got one then it can't be understood
That we are all united and together we are blessed
So we should stand together and just disregard the rest.

Somewhere Nice

Take me somewhere nice she said, a run out in the car
We'll go somewhere we've been before we needn't travel far
I want to see some places that meant such a lot to us
Take me somewhere nice she said, we could go on a bus.

I want to go somewhere with you where memories abound
And we could talk and reminisce on some familiar ground
I want to travel out with you before time drifts away
To take away our memories, please take me out today

I want to go somewhere with you, just you and me alone
Take me somewhere nice she said before the gap has grown
The gaps that destroys memories 'til they are cold as ice
Take me out today she said, please take me somewhere nice

So I took her somewhere nice we went to the country park
We set off in the morning and we didn't get home 'til dark
We saw the sun descending 'til it filled the sky with flame
When we got back home quite late she didn't know my name

Dream Lady Number Two

The lady who gives dreams came round
She came right in without a sound
And even though I slept so still
She bade me to obey her will
She took me by the hand and rose
And suddenly I wore my clothes
She took me to my children's houses
Where they were sleeping with their spouses
I saw their children in their beds
With shining hair surrounding heads
And then she bade me follow her
She gave no sign of when or where
I saw my love but young again
No graying hair no sign of pain
And then my father and my mother
With smiles to greet me like no other
Grandparents too I saw with glee
They smiled and grinned and looked at me
I saw old pets but in their prime
Not tarnished or pulled down by time
I saw my friends from school times days
Surrounded by a rosy haze
And places too for which I'd cared
And times and secrets never shared
She took me high within a cloud
And then we looked down at the ground
And higher still we travelled on
The sights and lights no longer shone
And then we came to a gate to see
She pointed out the way for me
She told me of the route to take
And then I knew I'd never wake

Busy Busy Me

There's lots to do when you retire
Like sitting quietly by the fire
And walking dogs, and stroking cats
And going out for daily chats.
There's books to read, newspapers too
You've quite a million things to do
Like watching cars out in the street
And wondering what next to eat
You sometimes make a shopping call
And wander round the shopping mall
And slowly walk not spending much
You're looking for the special touch
You take your shopping trip at noon
Lunch breakers have to be back soon
Can't understand why you are there
You're causing problems everywhere
You have to lie in bed quite late
To get you in a ready state
To rest most every afternoon
Because the evenings coming soon
You need to stop and drink some tea
About every hour from nine till three
And after that you need a break
Perhaps a sandwich and a cake
Holiday brochures you must peruse

So little time for you to lose
You have the time to sort the best
And leave the others for the rest
When holiday time arrives for you
You know exactly what to do
You pack your case or pack your trunk
And stay up late each night quite drunk
When catalogues arrive for seeds
You classify and sort your needs
It takes a lot of planning now
To get it right no matter how
We have all these great things to do
And many more I know that's true
For paid work time will not allow
We'll sort it out someday somehow

Grandpa's Cave

When he was just a little boy (that's what my Grandpa said)
He had a secret special cave behind the garden shed
And in this cave behind a rock there lived a dragon bold
And it was trained to warm the cave or so my Grandpa told

A passage led from in from the cave down to a coral beach
Where coconuts grew on the trees but all within his reach
And pineapples and strawberries and mangoes they all grew
It had a chocolate river and an ice cream fountain too

From off a passage in the cave just through a narrow crack
He often saw some polar bears and penguins white and black
They slid and skated on the ice and snow deep on the ground
And Grandpa watched them as he stood not making any
sound

He wrestled crocodiles one day and made them leave his
place
They rode his favourite elephant with lots of style and grace
He rolled the snakes to balls like string and bounced them out
of sight
And then he taught the birds to sing right through the day
and night

One day when Grandpa's not about I'm going to find his cave
I'll go and see the things he saw that is if I am brave
And when I do I'll tell Grandpa of what I've done and then
The two of us will visit and he'll think he's young again

Grandpa's Tree

In my grandpa's garden there's a really special tree
And high within its branches there's a platform just for me
I reach it from a ladder, which is really very high
And when I am stood at the top I sometimes touch the sky.

I look out from my special place and I can see the sea
With pirates chasing merchant ships but they don't frighten
me
I shout at them and wave my sword and they all sail away
I keep the ocean pirate free at least once every day.

Sometime when I see Africa I see the lions proud
They roll and scratch and stretch and growl so very very loud
I see giraffes sometimes also as they stroll all at the ease
They peer in to my tree at me but never eat its leaves

I see cowboys and horses as they chase Red Indian braves
And just before they leave my sight each cowboy stops and
waves
I sometimes see a waterfall where water falls for miles
And all the people watching it their faces filled with smiles

One day I saw a mountain peak all covered with ice and snow
The climbers striving for the top had not got far to go
I shouted out aloud to them and watched them plant their
flag
They'd carried it for miles and miles in a little yellow bag

My Grandpa says I fall asleep when I am up the tree
But he is snoozing in his chair and isn't watching me
He doesn't really know that I can see the things I do
I'm sure that if he ever knew then he would climb up too

The Ferryman to Hell

I dreamed I walked a stony path neath skies of almost black
No light to guide me on my way along this rugged track
Just howling winds and thunderous rolls to heed me on my
way
And yet I knew I must go on to reach my goal this day
At first the path was steeply made a climb to break the weak
But still I had to take that path and reach the highest peak
And when at last the summit reached I looked and saw below
There in a boat rocked by the waves was he I'd yet to know
This hooded creature raised his arm and beckoned me to go
And so I took the downward path to meet him down below
When I reached him and saw his shape no skin did I espy?
Just bones all clothed in deepest black and fire came from
each eye
You change your ways he hissed at me or with me you must
go
To where no friends you'll ever see and no one else will know
And from that time as I awoke I knew the answer well
The creature who had wanted me was the Ferryman to Hell
I recall now the smouldering eyes, the stench of rancid breath
And how his sight had filled my head with everlasting death
Oh let me dream no more like this a horror to endure
Was this a warning on my life I never will be sure?

I'll Leave The Light On

I'll leave the light on as I go and daylight slips away
Just a light to lift the evening's gloom
So if the Angels come for you and you are there alone
They'll see you lying quiet in your room
I know the Angels want you for to take you to their home
In that special place above the sky
And if they take you home with them away from all the pain
I'll try so very hard just not to cry
So as I turn to leave you after whispering my goodbye
I promise I'll be back just when I can
I'll keep your memory in my heart and send out thoughts of
love
For loving you has always been my plan
Then as I tiptoe from your room after a goodnight kiss
To give myself a long and lonely night
I'll leave the door slightly ajar so you won't feel alone
And I promise that I'll not put out the light.

Near Yet Far Away

Remembering just how things were
and memories hurt so much
Is when your love is far away
but close enough to touch
The light of love gone from their eyes
no knowing looks or smiles
That's when an arms length seems to be
a thousand empty miles
Oh that we could take illnesses
and lose them out in space
Just in the hope that it would bring
once more that loving face
But age and times goes rolling by
relentlessly it seems
And all the plans and hopes
are gone together with the dreams
It's just a plan life gives to you
until that final day
Your love is near enough to touch
but oh so far away

Walking Together

Oh that I could walk again just hand in hand with you
To places we had been before, to places that we knew
We'd see the places as we knew them many years ago
And feel the feelings that we had that gave us both that glow
The river with its grassy banks, the forest on the hill
The castle with it's tumbling walls where everything was still
The deer deep in the shrouded mists on Scotland's highest
peaks
The seagulls shrieking at the shore with ever open beaks
And children playing in the snow all wrapped to stand the
cold
The Sunday morning church service with people very old
The golden chicks with clucking hens parading in the spring
The joy of getting married with the bright new shiny ring
A baby in its cot so still and smelling warm and sweet
The joy of pushing out a pram just up and down the street
And taking kids to school each day to see them walking proud
And see them after school each day all shouting really loud
To see your children growing up to make their way in life
To see them settle down at last with husband or with wife.
Oh that we could walk again to see the things we knew
Perhaps when we shall meet again we'll share these things we
two.

The Shawl on the Chair

There's an old rocking chair with a shawl on the back
It's facing the window looking out on a track
The track to a farm far away on a hill
That's where this lady lived before she was ill
She was born on that farm where she lived all her life
Being baby and daughter and mother and wife
Till the kids all moved on and the spouse passed away
Leaving wonderful memories to think of each day
When they said she was ill to be taken in care
Her family came back and settled her there
She could just take a token they said and they left
And she took her old chair feeling lost and bereft
So she spent all her time rocking just too and fro
Looking right up the hill to the farm she loved so
Then one day she ceased rocking the chair became still
She had drifted away as she looked at the hill
Well her family came back just to do what they could
And they paid their respects, as a family should
But they left her old chair with the shawl on the back
Then they all went away and they never came back
Sometimes when the moon is quite bright in the sky
And casts a pale shadow you may wonder why
The shawl on the chair with its border quite plain
Sort of glows in the moonlight as the chair rocks again

No Sad Songs Please

I know things have been pretty rotten
And I'm trying to just get along
Whatever you do try to help me,
Don't let anyone sing a sad song
Play a tune full of laughs, make me giggle,
Make me roll on the floor full of glee
Don't show a sad film like a weepy,
That sort of thing's not for me
Make it rude make it coarse make it vulgar
I can take all these things in my stride
If somebody starts to shed teardrops
Then I'll go and probably hide
Lots of joy, lots of fun, loads of sniggers,
Spread them out, share them round I won't moan
I sing the sad songs and I play the sad films
When I'm tucked up in bed on my own

Once in a While

Once in a while will you think of me?
When I've gone and no longer around
Maybe a memory will come to you
Carried along on a sound
Perhaps it could be from a picture
From an album long since put away
Or from some shared anniversary
Remembered on some special day
Once in a while will you think of me?
And I'll come around you and then
I will be there and I'll wait for you
Till we're together again
Once in a while will you think of me?
Think of me kindly and smile
Send me your love, I'll send mine to you
Think of me once in a while

David Marland

I was born in Oldham in 1970 the youngest of five children I had many influences in growing up. Mainly trying to be different and not following the crowd but watching from a distance. School was hard but not as hard as the cane or the strap and I soon learned the quickest route to knowledge. Music was also a big influence when growing up the different styles and flavours of the seventies and eighties filled my head with a kaleidoscope of sounds. At the age of about thirteen I started to write short poems just for fun. Most of them just a play on words for example, if I was going to the corner shop for some cigarettes the line would be 'I am going to see shorner cop for some oily rags,' and so on. Only when I got older that I found the true power of words when I heard the early rap sounds from the U.S. and how the kids can be influenced with negative words looped together primitively. I consider my self to be a pretty laid back about most things but the one thing that fires my engines is injustice caused by greed. When something is so blatantly wrong and everybody sees it but money and greed force an opinion on everyone. Somebody once said the pen is mightier than the sword and I live by that rule. I pull a powerful word out of my head and assemble an army of them in the form of letter or poem. Then launch it as far as possible towards negative influences and greed in all directions because I am totally convinced of and steadfastly believe in the incredible power of words.

Christmas town

It's raining again in Christmas town
The lights have gone up and the rains coming down
People push to look with their hands in glove
Looking for things for the ones they love.

Silver and gold that's what's on my list
The man in the shop he will insist
To wrap it up in paper with a bow
Now I really have to go.

It's still raining in Christmas town
I'm stood outside and feeling down
The puddle on the path reflects the light
Now for a taxi I have to fight.

Shoppers rush past me
Just to be the first in the taxi
A car goes by and I get a puddle in the face
It's time to go and leave this place.

We are all wrapped up in this Christmas town
I'm getting out before I drown
It's all too much it's got to stop
The magic we seek is not in the shop.

It's in the face of a child with a smile
Not in this town with it's tacky style
The magic it's at home with your family and friends
All this sparkle it makes us pretend

When the fake magic leaves this place
It will leave behind two nasty tastes
Sickly sour debit and debt
Two flavours you can never forget.

Stamp Stone

The cane you used is now broken
The laws you obeyed are now changed
The hand you struck with is now withered
But your name and the face is the same

The face you saw was a stranger
The face I saw was yours
The standards you lived up to now bind us
Unable to shake off your ghost

The stone I look upon is yours
Stamped forever there is your name
The stone is in my shadow
But in my soul you will always remain

See-saw

From the biggest and the bluest sky
I fell into a storm cloud.
I grabbed it's silver lining then plummeted down
to ride on the crest of a wave.
Only to sink in the darkest of oceans,
then rescued by a smiling dolphin,
being chased by a ward of sharks.
I landed on a golden sandy beach,
and stubbed my toe on a rock.
To heaven and hell on the rollercoaster of love,
and you held my hand.

Pop Boom Bang

Onomatopoeia is the strangest word,
The strangest row of letters you ever heard,
It's the sound a word makes as it would appear,
POP BOOM BANG that's onomatopoeia.

It's the use of a word and the sound it imitates,
Like the BANG of doors and the SQUEAK of gates,
So listen carefully at a sound a word makes,
Like the HISS of steam and the SCREECH of brakes.

Horizontal Fall

On the horizon there is definitely something there.
Moving slowly at first but growing at every blink of an eye.
The wind of change is blowing as the horizon flashes blue,
red, yellow and green.
Bringing hope and promises to make the people happy and to
put wrongs right.
It is growing in immensity swamping every sense smothering
our day-to-day lives.
It is on every bill board and newspaper, it's on the radio and
television.
Today's the day its here,
Ready to burst,
Hold on tight,
Then it's gone,
The wind of change turned out to be.
The same old farts in different suits.
The party's over back on the horizon for another five years.
Running the country down and getting paid for it.

Follow the Bandera

I have travelled to Carnoustie and Nairn
Then on to each Loch in its turn
I have been to Urquhart at Ness
To see the heart of wilderness

I have tasted the purity of solitude
Then seen beauty with no interlude
So come while your heart escorts you
To the brave lands of Escotia

Say Something

Say something beautiful, say something sweet
Say something interesting that people will repeat
Words can be colourful words can be fun
Words can warm your soul… like the summer sun

So say something bright say something warm
So say something that won't cause a storm
Some words can be dark, some words can be cold
Some words are like poison, so I'm told

Everything you say needs to be right
Everything you say has to be bright
It all won't mean a thing this is well known
Because everything you say needs the right tone

Caterpillar Cat

Horace (the caterpillar) and Sally (the cat)
Sat under a tree and had a little chat
Sally asked: "Horace, do you want to play?"
Horace said: "No! Now go away"

"Pleeeeease!" said Sally, "I promise to be good."
"No!" said Horace. My place is under this wood!"
"Fine!" said Sally, "Horace, you're so rude!"
And with that, she went off to find some food.

"Wait!" said Horace, "I will play out very soon.
I can't just now, as I'm stuck in my cocoon!"
"Ok," said Sally, "Then we'll have to wait and see!
I'll climb up here and hide in this tree!"

Two days then went by while Horace stayed asleep.
Sally finally climbed on down to take a little peep.
She found Horace in the afternoon.
Very carefully she sniffed the cocoon.

"Boo!" said Horace, and flapped his brand-new wings.
"Wow!" said Sally, "But what are those things?"
"I'm a butterfly now," said Horace to the cat,
"I can no longer play with you and that's just that!"

"Pleeease!" said Sally, "Let's play and have some fun?"
"No!" said Horace – and flew off towards the sun.
Sally jumped up into the blue sky.
But Horace flapped his wings and said: "good bye"

The McHugh we knew

Billy McHugh came
Down from the hills
In the summer of
Nineteen hundred and two

From hills to mills
King Cotton called
The chimney bellowed and blew,

From mills to trenches
The English king called
To fight for something Billy never knew

From trench to mud
The good lord called
From Billy now poppys grew

From France to the highlands
Billy called out
I did it for them and for you

Somnia

Behind closed eye lids you will find a land. A place of
shadows, hills of monochrome and sky of sepia.
Rivers of black silk and open seas of the darkest oil silently
lap the grey sandy beaches.
In this land you will find a man wondering forever in this
darkened world searching endlessly turning over every rock,
stone and pebble.
The man carries with him a sack grey in colour a bulging in
volume.
Every ten miles the shadowy figure stops to dig at the dark
earth. Then franticly he starts to claw with his hands to reveal
a shining silver star.
He places it in his bag with the others again and again he
stops until he can carry no more.
He rests for a short while but his searching never stops.
His bag contains not jewels of precious metals but questions
and answers.
So if you find yourself in this land the man you will see is me
in somnia.

Replay

Bang went the swords of my brave men,
Crash they went as they echoed again,
Bang went the shields and one man yield,
On his aching knees in a muddy field,
With a braveness that boarded on insanity,
He stood slowly up and then ran at me,
Years and centuries these battles have been fought,
Some have been won and some have been bought,
As he ran at me with his broad sword waving,
I pulled out my white flag then gave in,
These are just toys and the steel isn't real.
I have to go now for my evening meal.
We are just playing a silly old game,
But over the years it's stayed just the same.

Moments of Wonder

When a child knows its mother
When a heart finds a home
When a soul finds a lover
Then a mind doesn't roam

When a child's mind starts to grow
When from the sky comes thunder
When from the north it starts to snow
Then every moment is a wonder

Friendship

Friendship is no good on your own
Reading old messages on your phone
It's up to you to make the move
Each day your friendship you have to prove
Now is the time don't be late
Don't hang about to find your mate
So go outside to find your buddy
Help each other play and get muddy
It's on each other you can rely
Play in the sun as the day goes by

Castle King

From the garret down to the gate
This is my home estate
From the chimney down to the drain
This is my own domain

It may only be a house in a red brick row
But there is one thing I do know
You can keep your euro and your pound
I am going to rule my home ground

I won't be lead like a somnambulist
By some namby-pamby by the wrist
I don't want to know about your exchange rate
So on your way out shut the gate

To the White Tower of Aldhulme

Tha was an owd man from owdum
Who went tu thee council an towed 'em
Thi town's a joke, every buggers broke
Sw wi back o' his hand he roled 'em

Sandra Rowell

My name is Sandra Rowell, and I am a wife, mother and grandmother. I am also a Costa Nominated author. I began writing as a child and found it an escape from the harsh realities of being a child in the 1950s and early 1960s. I write children's stories, poetry and novels and very much enjoy what I do. I don't see writing as a job, I see it as a pleasure and it's amazing how, at the end of a long day, you can feel relaxed and totally at ease just by writing.

It's also a way of getting rid of any frustrations you have. You can express all your feelings in poetry, anger, joy, sadness and loneliness, are all good reasons to write. I don't have a particular poet that inspires me to write, although I do enjoy reading poets like Keats, Wordsworth and even Shakespeare. Writing poetry allows you to escape into a world of fantasy as it allows the writer freedom to do whatever they like. I find that writing poetry helps me a lot especially if I am feeling sad, happy or just a little lonely.

My main goal in life is to be an inspiration to others, and if by writing poetry or novels does this then I am a success. It takes someone special to install values into others and if I can help people of any age and capabilities to realise a dream, and if you are prepared to put in a little hard work and effort, you too will have your dream. I am 55 years of age and it has taken me 30 of them to achieve my dream. It just goes to show, you are never too old to have a dream come true.

Seasons

The rain falls down so steadily
The wind it blows so fiercely
Scenes of winter fill my head
I think I'll stay in bed
Snug and cosy safe and warm
Safe from any harm

Springtime brings the flowers now
Myriads of colour, wow
Plenty of things for me to do
April brings the showers too
Young birds taking to the wing
Time for young lovers to sing

Next there is the summer sun
Fun and games for everyone
Children playing on the beach
Parents within easy reach
Lovers walking hand in hand
Just the way the good Lord planned

Last there is the autumn brown
Leaves are all falling down
Nights grow close and oh so dark
Lovers going for a walk
Another years has gone by
My, how the time does fly

A Face

A face can tell you many things
It opens its mouth when it sings
It cries, it laughs
It sheds tears too
It speaks to say I love you

Laughter lines appear around the eye
The eyes fill with tears and then they cry
A nose that tells you if something smells right
Ears that listen for noises in the night

A face will tell emotions true
There can be no fooling you
A mouth that speaks words and you will find
They can be both cruel and kind
The face is the greatest thing I know
Whatever you ask, it will tell you so

A Soldier's Tale

I joined as a lad to fight a war
Few would believe what I heard and saw
A flag flying high, a drummer boy beating
A whispered prayer or a friendly greeting
A gun being fired from land or sea
A bullet surely meant for me

I move just in time so the bullet goes past
I offer a prayer that my luck will last
I hear a shout, someone's been hit
I cringe as I feel the pain of it
There is no safety here on the ground
And I pray that soon we will be found

The night grows dark, I can barely see
Will someone be coming for me
I watch and wait with gun in hand
My legs so stiff I cannot stand
I cannot hear, I cannot see
Is there something wrong with me

A medic comes to see me at last
And I believe my pain has past
I cannot feel my body now
There is no pain anyhow
A whispered prayer, a sweet goodbye
And it is my turn to die

A Lost Love

As I lay dreaming in my bed
Thoughts of you came into my head
A twinkle of a star at night
Makes me want to hold you tight
And as I'm drifting off to sleep
Memories of you I'll keep

I awake next day with you still there
All around me, in the air
I yearn to hold you in my arms
The love we shared still keeps me warm
A photograph of you I keep
Close beside me as I sleep

I whisper your name but you're not there
No longer with me anywhere
Your face again I'll never see
Never lying close to me
A silent prayer I offer you
Hoping that my wish comes true

Death has taken you from me
Together someday I know we'll be
Until then my love I know
From my heart you'll never go
As I lay dreaming in my bed
Thoughts of you stay in my head

The World

Many times I sit and wonder
What this world is all about
Some times I sit so quiet
Other times I want to shout
It's like I want to ask the world
What are you all about

Are you the Sun and Moon
Are you the stars in the sky
Are you the heart of the ocean
Or the rivers running by
Are you a rainbow full of colour
You are unlike any other

Are you the tides that turn the water
Are you the wind that blows the trees
Are you the rain falling in puddles
Or are you like me, all in a muddle

I ask myself these questions
Each and every day
I want to understand you
In each and every way

Sometimes I ask the question
What is the world about
It is then that I realise
It's about life, without a doubt

Empty Heart

A heart so full of emptiness
A heart so full of pain
Tears are constantly falling
Will I ever find love again

A tender look is needed
A glance or a kiss or two
I want so much to know my love
If my heart belongs to you

A silent prayer is offered
A wish for a dream to come true
I long to hold you in my arms
And share my love with you

My heart is full of emptiness
My heart is full of pain
My tears are constantly falling
No, I will never love again

Life

Life goes by in a whisper
It takes no time at all
A wink of the eye
A raindrop from the sky
Another soul is called

Take each day as it comes
Live and love as if it's your last
Don't ever dwell on problems
Don't ever live in the past

Be happy and smile each day
Don't let a teardrop fall
If you try not to worry
It takes longer for the reaper to call

There's a time for every emotion
A time to live and love
A time to laugh and cry
A time to suffer and a time to die
Don't let life pass you by

A Mother's Tears

The rain falls down as tears
As the battle begins to rage
It is a time of sorrow
Of bloodshed, horror and rage

The fields are full of bodies
The dead and the dying
A mother sits on the sidelines
All alone and quietly crying

She sees her son alone and lying
On the battlefield among the torn
She sheds a silent tear
As she recalls the day he was born

She waits for him to stir himself
But he lies so very still
She know by now that he is dead
So to stir he never will

A mother's tears are falling
As she hears her lost son call
Mother, oh mother where are you
I can't see your face at all

The day grows dark and dismal
As the rain clouds gather
It washes away the pain and blood
But still she sits there sighing

Rain falls down as tears
As the battle has ceased to rage
A mother sits quietly crying
And waits for the pain to ease

Little Witches

Spells and potions, magic too
These all make a witches brew
Toils and troubles, boils and bubbles
These all get you into muddles

Big pot burning on a fire high
Flames reaching high up to the sky
Nights as black as a coal oven
Meetings of the witches coven

Stars all shining in the sky
Black hat standing very high
Little kitten black as jet
Sitting as the witches pet

Children sitting in a row
Watching the fire all aglow
Halloween is here once more
Trick or treating galore

Little witches faces glowing
Tiredness, their bodies slowing
Time to do what mother said
Time to go back home to bed

Life Gone By

Dreams of a childhood forgotten
Life as it was years ago
Happiness, sadness, tears aplenty
A world that seemed to go so slow
A wish for the years to fly
Oh, to be an adult you sigh

To do whatever you want is fine
Go to work, have fun, and stay out late
To party and wine and dine with friends
To even go out on a date
A wish for the years to slow a little
It's great to be an adult, you sigh

You grow, marry and have a family
Children all around your feet
Now's the time for you to worry and fret
There's no way time can retreat
A silent wish for the years to linger
Lift as an adult is complete

Children grow into new adults
You watch as they all leave home
You remember the days you had as a child
Times that you cannot repeat
A wish for the clock to turn backward
Oh, to be a child again, you sigh

Life's End

Lights at the end of a tunnel
A vision of times gone by
Dreams of things long forgotten
Where will we end up, you and I

A world we seem to have lost
Our old eyes see things long past
Our mind wanders far, far away
Thought we would never last

Heaven beckons us closer
The days grow dark and dim
Life grows ever shorter
As old age creeps further in

The summer of life is past now
The winter grows ever near
Old age has come a calling
Death is closer I fear

Our days of youth are over
Life as we know comes to an end
Listen to all the angels
Come home is the message they send

At last I close my eyes now
Heaven's gates are open for me
No more will I walk the streets of earth
No more pain or heartache will I see

There is no want or hunger
Happiness is all around
My time on earth is over at last
Death has come calling for me

Light

Light floods in through the windows
Bringing a new born day
It brightens up the darkness
And takes all our troubles away

Light can come in many forms
The sun, a bulb or a torch
It shines in all of our homes
And even on the front porch

Some people are afraid of the darkness
Some people are scared of the night
But everyone welcomes the morning
Everyone welcomes the light

We can be sad when the weather is dark and bad
But the sunshine lights up the sky
The light makes us smile again
But the rain can make us cry

I love to live in the daylight
And not like a mole underground
A smile on my face, a song in my heart
Keeps the light all around me I found

The Ocean

Out on the ocean down among the deep
Fishes swim together without appearing to sleep
The water drifts high above them
I wonder what other secrets it keeps

The waters seem to go on forever
Never reaching the end of the world
A bed that's nothing but shells and sand
Coral, pearls and shipwrecks, but no land

A ship can sail on the ocean
Sailing to far away lands
Battles have raged on their waters
Ships have sunk in their sands

The ocean is big, deep and beautiful
Blue from beginning to end
Aeroplanes fly high above them
Across their waters love and hope can be sent

Although I love the ocean
I think I'll stay on dry land
I have not got fins for swimming
That's not the way I'm planned

Water Water

Water, water everywhere
And lots of it to drink
It runs out through the taps
And down the kitchen sink
Rain comes down in drops
And more water hits the ground
It runs into the rivers
And covers all of the land
Floods can damage houses
Crops and property too
We use it to wash ourselves
And also to flush the loo
We boil it for cooking food
We use it to have a shower
Its often taken for granted
But it has a lot of power
There is no doubt about it
Water is oh so good
We cannot live without it
I doubt we ever could

Call of the Wild

Hear the whistle of the wind
As it blows through the earth
Down below in the valleys
And high in the treetops

Birds flying high on the wing
Just listen as they sing
The fishes in the stream
As they silently swim

Copses and green hedges
Where all sorts of animals rest
Mother nature is unbroken
And put to the test

Volcanoes erupting and stars shining brightly
High in the sky twinkling nightly
The call of the wild
As the world spins again

Mountains so high with their snow topped peaks
Night turns to morning as the dawn comes creeping
The world wakens again to another day
The call of the wild begins again

Alan Barker

I was born in Richmond, North Yorks, in 1951. My father was in the army stationed at nearby Catterick and as a family we followed dad around the world to his many postings. Aden, Cyprus, Germany (twice!) and Northern Ireland were amongst some of the countries we visited. This had an effect on us as three sons followed dad into the services. I was the black sheep; I joined the Royal Navy whilst the other two boys went into the army. I served in the Fleet Air Arm for twelve years, working as an electrical mechanic on jets and helicopters. This stood me in good stead when I left the RN in 1978 and joined a helicopter company at Dyce heliport, where I still work as an avionics engineer on the helicopters that service the North Sea rigs. Those military connections have left me with a deep abiding passion for military history, especially that of the First World War, and this is evident in the poems I write about the carnage of the four long years of the war on the Western Front. My dear long-suffering wife and two children will testify to that but at least I make buying my birthday or Christmas present easy to choose! Poetry is a great medium for telling a story and that's what I try to do with my work, whether it's a war poem or a simple verse about family life as I see it. I hope that in these pages you can find something that makes you stop and think. If it does I've succeeded in what I set out to do when I sit down and write.

Longing

Don't search for me in some far away place.
Don't look for my smile, on a stranger's face.
Rather, seek me out in the summer sky
Hear my voice in a curlew's cry.

Don't yearn for me when the year falls round.
Nor see my footprints in fresh-tilled ground.
Instead, hear my laugh in a tumbling stream
My presence will soothe, in a warm-filled dream.

No sadness, tears, no time to grieve.
I live all around, in the air that you breathe.

Shellshock

If I could talk, what tales I'd tell,
of broken guns and putrid flesh.
Each twisted corpse a poppy sell
so planting shattered minds afresh.
With memories of their recent hell.

If I could see where once men stood
and fought. The clinging stench of war.
Ploughed fields now rotted, foul-some mud.
I'd turn and flee to whence before,
the world no longer stank of blood.

If I had strength enough to crawl,
in cover. There with fumbling breath.
This choking ease by letting fall,
the rifle. Instrument of death.
Then rising, scream, "Where are you all?"

Forgiveness 1916

Forgive me all my tears, my mind is weary,
For those I loved, now gone into the night.
Freed of all their earthly fears. And dreary.
Whose passing marked the drawing down of light.
Forgive me my response, my heart is sore,
Youth's needless sacrifice, to right a wrong.
And life? I loved it once, 'til clouds of war.
When Spring meant warmth. And flowers.
And sweet birdsong.

My Valentine. Feb 14th

Would that I could kiss your pain away,
and bring the warm sun back into your life.
Then, hands entwined, wander down some leafy lover's lane.
With my best friend, partner, lover and wife.
In looking back, I could not choose,
another one to share the many miles.
By loving you I'd speak such words as no-one else could use.
And view the world through our children's smiles.

Empty Fields and Lives.

The fields are fallow, empty now, now all our young men have fled. Gone for soldiers on other's soil, gone to the war in the west. Where summer's harvest gaily trampled, with marching songs and jest. Harbours a ripened seasonal crop, whose furrows and ditches run red. A pigeon calls in a ghostly copse, shadows lengthen on untilled ground. Abandoned ploughshares rusting lie, cracked in an overgrown yard. Once-gleaming metal scoured and blackened, leather split shiny and hard. And cobwebs dance a different tune, to the distant, muttering sound. A photograph solemnly stares in the hall, the boy/man now passed from our sight. Hounds warmed by the fireside, ears cocked, wait in vain. For the echo of footsteps and familiar voice, which will never be heard again. As gunfire rattles the windowpanes, far into the deepening night. This land, our land, lies barren and bare, mute homage to honour and trust. The fruits of its offerings left no seed to sow. Whilst in Flander's abundance the poppies, blood red, scarlet, wantonly grow. Our love, our lives, our hopes all gone. In some foreign field, long crumbled to dust.

Sniper 1915

Toss a penny, toss a penny.
Heads or tails, there isn't any
time to lose, to cross that gap.
Clutch your rifle, jam your cap
on tight. Now run, it's easy see?
Quickly, mate, just follow m...

A Tyneside Shanty

Tall, proud iron ships that slid straight down the slips
To the sound of loud cheering, from thousands of lips.
The riveter's hammers, that rang out in time
Now rusting lie quiet, beneath rubble and slime.

The cranes in the docks point their jibs to the sky.
In seeking an answer of men who asked: "Why?"
Where has the skill gone that was once yours and mine?
Away with the flotsam that floats down the Tyne.

We built them, those ships, built for peace and for war.
With love and with pride, like our fathers before.
Then watched as they sailed for lands we'd never see
Some bringing back cargoes, some keeping men free.

From Elswick to South shields we'd orders to fill.
From a world full of awe at our craft and our skill.
Where now is the fame that was once yours and mine?
Long sailed out to sea, on the tide with the Tyne.

The screeching of gulls where men's voices once cried.
Are the yesteryear ghosts that now haunt Tyneside.
The shipyards long gone, to marinas and docks.
Bear no trace of the masts that stood tall on the stocks.

A few rotted timbers half buried in mud,
sad reminders of power, 'ere the tide starts to flood.
Where has our past gone, that was once yours and mine?
Intermingled with tears and the taste of the Tyne.

Culloden

Called Drummossie moor

There they stood, a world apart.
Arrogant, haughty, swathed in red.
Cannon-shot and musket ball.
Deadly. Whirring overhead.
Grim-set faces, no compassion.
Pitiless, they wished us dead.

Here we stood, upon our honour.
On this moor, this blood-soaked field.
Cornered as a stag at bay.
The aim of hatred, ill-concealed.
Proudly then our banners fluttered.
Passion to our foes revealed.

Wreathed in smoke we charged in vain,
the hopes of Scotland dashed before.
The pike and bayonet, burnished steel.
Recoiled as foam upon the shore.
Whilst falling back, left of our kin.
In tangled heaps to rise no more

Ashen-faced we stumbled past,
the form of him who once would reign.
Behind, the butchery began.
Foul deeds that blacken Albion's name.
In bog and heather now we hide.
Until our Charlie comes again.

To my son

I held you naked in my arms and wept
Tears of joy coursed freely down my face
Emotionally drained by your witnessed birth
Watched closely as you slept
Blankets creased up, huddled, in place

Dreaming of the time
When I would show you the world
Its sights, sounds and never ending sky

Your hair, dark hair, matted on my arm
Wet, tightly curled
And we'd see it all together
You and I

Fiercely I'd protect you
Keep the wolves from our door
Making you safe
In the harbour of my arms until death

All of these promises I made you
And much, much more
Whilst I rocked you to sleep
Fingers gripping my thumb
Inhaling your milk-sweet breath

Eventually, I laid you back down
Reluctantly, and stayed a while longer
To softly stroke your head
Then quietly left as I'd crept in, without a sound

Leaving you with the legacy of my love
For the long, long years ahead.

Innocence

How many nights, when just a boy
I'd lay curled up inside my bed
Listening to the thunderous roar
Of engines flying overhead

And running to the window
Glimpsed the shadows of the bomber's flight
In all their metalled multitudes
Death-laden fleets that pierced the night

Whose passing left me naught but pride
A young boy's head filled with the lies
Of men and politician's hate
Which sent our youth to darkened skies

The fear and pain was theirs alone
A parachute's silk white as the shroud
Where hunters stalked their prey on high
Stark silhouettes against the cloud

The shattered town's crazed funeral pyres
Such nightmare sights I never saw
Nor cried as silent witness to
The empty futility of war

Up, up aloft
Whilst young men fought
and died and cursed and wept
Far, far below.
I slept

Life's Passage

We'll meet again. In the warmth of the sun
In some other dimension, some other place
Feather-soft memories of far-away dreams
Whispering echoes too distant to trace

Time frightens me, the swift relentless
Passage of the quiet, noiseless days
Seconds blurring quickly to countless hours
Changing our lives, in other ways

Years that race by in the blink of an eye
Denoting the season's progression at pace
The worth of our souls worn for all to take note
Laughter lines on a face

Paint your picture on this, life's canvass
Daub, splash bright hues as an artist possessed
Then colour my heart with the tale of our years
And love me, for all the time we have left

A Fisher's Tale

When will the fair winds blow me straight to your side
On a storm-tossed sea, by an incoming tide
When I'll swear to stay close, yet 'til morning just bide
And then leave you alone to your sleeping
For all that I love, it's the sea that I've wed
Where the wind in my face lets the sail have its head
Takes me far, far away from the warmth of our bed
Where I can't hear the sound of your weeping
Didn't I swear on my knees, its not me you should marry?
For a man such as I is not one who could tarry
When a wind from the west brings a wave that can carry
Me off, with a prayer, in God's keeping
So forgive and forget me and draw down the shade
To keep out the night as the day's last lights fade
Not allowing the memories of the life we once made
In that sad, lonely heart come a-creeping

The Living Years, 1973-84

Their rooms echo eerily, empty now
Where have they gone?
Those children of ours and the years?
How did they vanish?
Is all that is left their memories
and unshed tears?
Sunlight falls on unfilled beds
Where is the laughter?
The sense of joy and the fun?
Ghostly footsteps, replaced by a man
Where once stood our son
How time has stretched, will they ever return?
The hopes of our future
And our lives
Can life still carry on when those children become
Husbands and wives?

Year's End

See me.
The falling leaves of autumn.
Red-russet, golden brown, black.

Dying.

Whirling and swirling.
Vast armies. Hosts.
Soft-carpeted

Lying.

Feel me.
Crisp underfoot.
Deep trodden.
By days last light,
windblown, airborne

Flying.

Hear me.
In swathes stirring
restlessly. Shimmering
Dirt-mantled, rustling

Sighing.

Personal Loss

On searching for an answer why;
The world's become a dark and silent place
Whilst youth shrinks back in shadows,
Fearful of the storm to come
My mind, beset with memories,
Tries to come to terms and trace
The starting point in whose will this was done

A brighter star I never saw,
A kinder word I never knew
Your gentle ways I thought would
Charm Death's hold
From paths you trod
Where is the sense?
In whose defence must land
The pain of losing you?
I cannot say
My faith is gone
There is no God

Farewell

Dearest mother,

      Whilst writing this I cannot stray too far. The coming light of day will dawn, and death earth's beauty mar. Around the sleeping men bestir. Who knows when rest they'll find again? Beyond the silent, misty morn, will lives still be as once they were? Or stay the way they are? Far from our sight the farmyard wakes. A herdsman, yawning lends a hand. To aid the life the farmer makes. The cattle low, a strutting cockerel cries. As all around, in this rich land, we gather up our arms to pray. That God will safely see us through, our fear of pain and death allay. A distant *thud!* A soldier dies.

      Fresh blood spilt on this soil anew, to feed the sorrow of the heart that breaks.

      I must go now, a promise keep, to fight our foe, and if God wills, to find a different kind of sleep.

Your loving son
William.

To The memory of Sgt J W 'Will' Streets, 12th York and Lancaster Regiment (Sheffield City battalion.) Killed in action at Serre, on the Somme, 1st July 1916.

Hope

I, in this trench can see him still, a lark in all his ecstasy. And know that through God's grace I will, remain in peace, at liberty. To sit and watch the bird o'erhead, to sense delight in all he sings. So listening, ache for those abed, at home, who sleep. A thousand things, that come to mind as I dream on, unburdened as the bird above. Whilst here below, a different song, has displaced honour, trust and love. The coolness of the early morn is shattered by the daily strafe of shells. Which leave men mangled, torn, no trench too deep, no funkhole safe enough to keep the firestorm out, the minds unfettered by the din. Of Death's triumphal, gleeful shout, blood harvest to his grasp drawn in. We stooping, crouch, like burdened beasts, the years turned bitter by man's hate. This world has seen a myriad feasts. Despoiled while Hell's doomed armies wait. Yet, pale, amongst this earthly toil, 'midst all this horror, pain and strife. A cornflower buds on sanguine soil. Sweet flowers of the trenches, you bring me back to life.

The last line is taken from Sgt 'Will' Street's letter home in 1916, which inspired this poem.

Andrew Powell

I was born in 1984 in the City of Sunderland, England. It is a red and white city and I, as a resident, have a red and white heart. Writing became a big part of my life around two years ago. To me it is an expression, an enjoyment and a river in which the creative waters of my mind can flow with liberty and pleasure. Three of my favourite poets are T.S Eliot, Robert Browning and Edgar Allen Poe although I do not think any single individual inspired me to start writing (poetry or novels) because I believe that inspiration is a chemical devised in the human mind for ones own need rather then that of another influence. I suppose, to me, inspiration is just a pseudonym for ambition and it is with these factors that creativity spawns and thrives. Like all men should have, I have my priorities in strict order and assembled in line of importance. My two wonderful children come first and my life runs around them. Writing slots nicely into the gaps of free time in-between. They are the foundation on which my life is built and it will always be that way. I believe that love is the wage of life and parenthood is therefore the occupation. We all go through times of happiness and sadness, our lives are symbolized by the two states of emotion, and sometimes we need a voice to express our feelings of both. Poetry, for me, is that voice and I for one am glad that you - as the reader - are willing to listen.

A Bleak Awakening
Field of shattered hope (Part 1)

Pigeons with burning tail feathers
Fly over head into the blustering wind
As embers depart into their wicked wake.
Flying not west but away from their tales.

The smoke trail forms and follows
I see, watching from my mind.
Planted in this grey sand beach
As the birds and wind wail wild.

An endless snaking shore line ravels
And travels up the ghost grey coast.
The black tar or oil riddled tide washes up
Coating a mantle upon its host.

Eternal burning fires
Dully illuminate this lightless world.
Constantly existing under nightfall
Is this charred, black, immoral pearl.

No boat will ever appear on its horizon
No light afloat out on this sea, bar the
Fires that burn in smidgens on this black yonder
No one out there to rescue me.

There are two time bands within this land
The past and the present they are.
No future to prophet upon this kingdom
So I think back upon my past
And my journey so far…

The Less Lands of Lull
(Part 2)

Awoke amongst a pit of bones
A Golgotha of my family past
A migraine in my skull thumps and groans
From over the muddy banks I hear a rasp

Lacking hydration and salvation
I climbed that miry incline
Glanced a look over the crest and
Saw the reverse of a chest, a man's spine

Arched over naked in a bow
A rotten chassis health could not overthrow
His voice as hoarse a crow's, he spoke
'This way, Lull. That way, Lull, go!'

Made way across a land so bleak
Flat, empty earth felt hot and steep
Walked for hours before I reached its peak
And from the border, Lull I viewed

Spires, structures, edifices stemmed up and up
The tops piercing clouds of unfathomable smoke
That covered the kingdom like ozone, seemingly
A solo breath from the rooftops would choke

Below that constant black cloud
An eerie city lay in wait.
The hope of finding help arose
But open was its truth, for me to debate.

Reached and breached the city streets
Silence spoke among the buildings
A shot and a shrill squeal rang out
That rattled my sanity and my fillings

Confrontation arrived on main road
With a one eyed man waving a gun
Spoke an order to leave before the shells explode
Against he who trespasses in wretched Lull

That individual eye could not lie
It had tried to hide uncertainty and fear
I told how priority had been to pass by
Leaving, wondering if he arrived like I, here

The black heart of Lull I came
There I met a father shivering in a box
Who offered me a space next to him
I entered into this good man's box

I awoke later, hands bound together taped
He offered his kindness under sly ambitions of rape
Struggled and kicked and struggled
Desperation intense, intently to escape

A boot struck viciously at his neck
And with a wretched snap
Granted had been the wish to escape
And escape he did, for now...

Past and present with nothing ahead
(Part 3)

The last normal scenario I remember
Was not a sight to be admired
The smell of burning rubber
The screech of skidding tires

The crashing thud of denting metal
The cracking clash of breaking glass
Of a head bulleting through a windshield
In an unexpected crash

Grey figures becoming fainter
Gathered in a ring above
Red silhouettes they turn
For now I see through blood
And then the world turned blank...

...Until I awoke into that pit
Amongst bones of my past
From there I quest to here, this shore
Where I will sit forever...
With shattered hope!

Dreaming of Clouds

Different shapes, sizes & colours are clouds
Floating way up in the air.
You see black clouds floating with white clouds
But they never seem to stay there.
Maybe the odd few do, but the rest create tension.
Black & white clouds separate without word or mention.
But the grey clouds want to see:
The black and white clouds mix and stick together
As I write this poem,
My mind's not set on the weather.

For you, friend.

We all have roads to walk in life,
But yours was not too smooth.
Despite the bad things in your road,
You still knew how to groove.

A drink in one hand, dancing,
With a lady on your arm.
So wild, so mad and funny,
Yet so friendly and so calm.

A circle of us talking, standing,
Taking up the bar.
Thinking back to those times now
It seems unreal and far.

It would be good to live them over
And rehearse the times we had.
There's people who would argue
But I knew you were a good lad.

You made us smile and I can't count
The times you made me laugh
I hope one day I'll bump into you
On God's peaceful, heavenly, path.

Thanks to you I'll probably laugh and cry
Every time I hear Adagio for strings,
And there's only a chosen few of us
Who know the memories it brings.

So now I know that God was bored
And needed some entertainment...
Well Mellow...I hope he knows how wild
Things are going to get up there...

In memory of a best friend, a great lad and
a true 'good time guy'.
We thank you, we love you...but mostly, we miss you.

R.I.P Mark 'Mellow' Henson 1985 - 2008

A City Of Two Halves

A park with blooming beauty
Flowers sprouting from brown soil
The smell of mown grass tangy
As the stream trickles in toil.
A back alley spewing rancid odour
Mephitic reek commands the air
Urine stains the walls so dour
The typical scent of a muggers lair.
Restaurants, clubs, exclusive pubs
Radiant smiles upon the children's faces
High profile developments
But only regenerating central places.
Effete houses boarded shut
Rooftops gaping from the blazes
Littered gardens overgrown
A wasteland of wasted spaces.
To sunder means to split
Sunderland therefore means divided lands
After reading my description
I hope that now you understand.

Life's Reasons

The sun rolled down the Western sky
And kissed the surface of the sea
Perfection it is, I see, but only
Because you're here with me
Above, a sheet of stars mask the heavens
And dew becomes a gentle presence
Yet I feel saturated in crisp daylight
Due to your affectionate presence
Your will to live conducts and imprints
Itself upon my philosophy of life
And the reason I'm, here to watch the sun and stars
Is because I have you as my wife

If living needs a reason
Surely you are it

En Route To Liberty, I Be

I yield a sword of compromise
A weapon of new peace
To lay a law of justice
And spare the weak of their demise

Jingle of the bridle, giddy - giddy
Horse back across the plains
En route to an un-marshalled village
Cometh, a figure of law and no pity

For, all who sin here
Will shake hands with thy sword
With the hilt rimmed with ethics of thy Lord
And punished rightfully without falling tears

A free spirit of diplomacy I be
Cruising on a path of no destination
While searching with
My drawn sword of liberty

Yet I introduce liberty
To every place I reach
No rules will remain in my wake
And that is the law of the land

You're As

As tranquil and as gentle
As days first drops of dew
As beautiful and delicate
As petals freshly grew

Amazing and inspiring
Like the world's most graceful sight
Calm but simply mind-blowing
Like a sheet of stars at night

As easy and as smooth
As phonetics softest sound
As precious and as rare
As any diamond ever found

As this, as that…
What matters is AS you are
I am as proud as I can be of you both
As you are daddy's little stars.

A Path Lost

Are open arms sufficient
To embrace the feel?
Are they there anyway?
Are they real?
What is this feeling
That hampers down my chest?
Why does it persist to
Choose me as its nest?
And when will it spread
It's wings and move on?
When will it depart and
let my emotions return to best?
Does the world go on?
In this bleak dimension
I hope so, yet I think not
Yet the answer is as clear as thought
Which is belated to say the least
Like yeast in an oven
My willpower will rise
If only to fight an eternal war
No scars will remain in its wake
Unless the parasite gets its own way
Should I fight?
Or should I simply fall victim
To what feels like the unbeatable?
The issue in truth is debatable
Yet my mind, despite its drab state says:
Yes!
Why surrender?

No joy was ever won
By the elevation of a white flag
But no peace nor serenity
Was ever gained by battle
It is a no win situation!
A vile and noxious situation!
A situation created by our own
Ridiculous desires and
Disappointments and our own
May I say, unrealistic infatuation!
What walks us into this sullied path
Does not grasp our hand and lead us out
No!
We stand alone to find our way
From this wretched woodland
Many, never to be seen
Again!
Yet I remain hopeful of
Stepping drearily out of that
Dark forest and into the
Crisp brilliance of daylight
And as I approach the final furlong
Of this unholy state
I shall hope with the power
Of normality that
I step into the comfortable embrace
Of real, open arms
And there I shall bask until
The dark bird returns!

Mr Enchantment

I met a man of magic
In him; I did not believe
Until he waved his magic wand
And pulled a rabbit from his sleeve.

His face howled with laughter
His eyes cased a brilliant green glow
They made me feel surreal
While I watched this strange mans show.

Next out came a turtle
Music playing from it's shell
When he snapped his fingers so
It brought a tasty roasting smell.

From mid air he snapped a sandwich
That he gave me and I ate
From then on in his magic
Played a part upon my fate.

I met him in my 30's
Futures memories I now hold
Because when I walked away
I was only 9 years old.

A Predicting Brain

(Read fast and don't stop)

I cnat beleive I'm albe to raed what I'm wirting.
The way yuo cnat beleive taht yuo can raed it too.
I wirte in the nmae of laerning and not to cofnuse yuo.
Its wierd how yuo raed tihs wehn its not splet the same.
It sohws yuo how prdectiblity helps yuo run yuor brain.

How, when & why?

I look up and wonder:
How, when and why?

Do you realise how amazing it is
When looking at the sky?

How did the stars get there?
And what is at the end?

I can't even start to imagine what
It's too much to comprehend.

When was it created?
And when will it be gone?

Because everything that's born
Has to one day move along.

Why is it so beautiful
Yet so vastly ignored?

Something so tranquil and astonishing
Could only be created by a Lord!

The most amazing sight on Earth…
is right above you.

Dreamcatcher

[Extracted from little Jimmy's diary - 24th Dec 07]

I put a dreamcatcher above my bed last night
It brings me a more peaceful state of sleep
Now I manage to sleep the full length of the night
Without stirring or making a peep.

It hangs there with its feathers hanging
Its web weaved together good
Vital to me having better dreams
Without my father's fists drawing my blood.

Is it in a psychological or physical way?
Or does it fool and trick my mind?
I pray to God it helps me again
Coz the rest of the world has turned so blind.

So Santa all I ask of you
Is change my daddy from a fool
I beg, I beg, I beg of you
God! I don't want to get hurt.

One Hell of A World

I

Oppressive world,
Why choose I to rest
Your burden weight
Upon my rickety shoulders?

II

Ironic, for my shoulders
Stem arms and hands
That already carry deleterious
Bags of your luggage.

III

To live is not divine
But to survive is
For the weight and price
Is lethally crushing.

IV

For each second I spend upon you
Your logic becomes more enigmatic
Reasons for such obscurity
I feel my mind can't grasp it.

V

Thank you yonder around me
Thank you wretched rock of twirl
For now I have an understanding
Of why you're one hell of a world.

Never No Good

Daddy's slogging buckets of sweat out
While working too many hours
His wage barely pays the rent out
Forget buying mummy flowers

Saving up for Christmas
To fulfil his daughter's wish list
Wanting only to make her happy
He did not click he picked the old list

Spending all his hard earned money
On articles he thinks she wants
While she thinks Dad is a waste of space
As she desires getting what she wants

Come the 25th she opens her gifts without a smile
There's not the one she wanted so his selfish daughter cries
Now dad feels as low as his self esteem
He should not have to though, she is nineteen!

'Princess, what are you crying for?'
'Coz this isn't the new phone out!'
All he can say in his crestfallen voice is:
'But sweetie, it's the thought that counts.'

Two pebbles

Two pebbles on a beach
Either pebble, either end.
One pebble in the roughest rocks
One pebble in the golden sand.

Then the tide comes washing in
Picking the pebble up with force
Washing it down the beach
Depositing it in the rocks of course.

The pebbles sit side by side
Waiting upon the next strong tide
But mix and move with chemistry
Two pebbles from the same blue sea.

The pebbles feel a special link
These pebbles float and did not sink.
Then just as the two were getting on
Along came the tide and moved one on.

O' my Juliet

O' my Juliet,
How can one be so true?
I ask the starlit sky above
As I wish upon them, for you!

O' my Juliet,
Why must I be forced to live
When I don't have you to embrace
Or bask in the love you give!

Why oh why must I,
Feel the way I do when I meet you
I try to fight it
Fight I will, yet win I can't!

Perfection is an art
And art is a gift
That is true
As true as you!

O' my Juliet
You epitomise everything gracious
Everything complete
And everything eventual!

O' my Juliet
Have I ever bared witness to tears of joy?
Not until I saw your face
And listened to the adoration of life from your lips

I call for you in my mind
In my mind I call, I call
Yet nothing comes my way
But love never gives up, like I, for you!

From my window
The moon and stars I see
And I hope somewhere you sit as I do
Seeing the way that I see!

I envision, dare I say dream?
That one day, you will run to me
Running, your arms splayed with love
And into you I fall with grace!

And on your chest I will lay
Until I am physically forced to move
Because with you is where
I desire to spend the rest of my days!

O' my Juliet
I love you my Juliet
O' I love you, I do
You Juliet, you!

Other Titles From Cauliay Publishing

Kilts, Confetti & Conspiracy *By* Bill Shackleton
Child Of The Storm *By* Douglas Davidson
Buildings In A House Of Fire *By* Graham Tiler
Tatterdemalion *By* Ray Succre
From The Holocaust To the Highlands *By* Walter Kress
To Save My father's Soul *By* Michael William Molden
Love, Cry and Wonder Why *By* Bernard Briggs
A Seal Snorts Out The Moon *By* Colin Stewart Jones
The Haunted North *By* Graeme Milne
Revolutionaries *By* Jack Blade
Michael *By* Sandra Rowell
Poets Centre Stage (*Vol One*) *By* Various poets

Books coming soon

Underway—Looking Aft *By* Amy Shouse
The Fire House *By* Michael William Molden
The Upside Down Social World *By* Jennifer Morrison
The Strawberry Garden *By* Michael William Molden

All the above titles are available directly from Cauliay Publishing, from your local bookstore or from most Internet outlets.

Printed in the United Kingdom
by Lightning Source UK Ltd.
136214UK00001B/4-63/P